This book belongs to

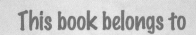

...a boy who wants to
discover his Bible

A BOY'S GUIDE TO DISCOVERING HIS BIBLE

JIM GEORGE

HARVEST HOUSE PUBLISHERS
EUGENE, OREGON

Cover by Dugan Design Group, Bloomington, Minnesota

Cover photos © NickS, carlosalverez / iStock

A BOY'S GUIDE TO DISCOVERING HIS BIBLE
Copyright © 2015 Jim George
Published by Harvest House Publishers
Eugene, Oregon 97402
www.harvesthousepublishers.com

Library of Congress Cataloging-in-Publication Data
   George, Jim, 1943-
   A boy's guide to discovering his Bible / Jim George.
      pages cm
   ISBN 978-0-7369-6254-4 (pbk.)
   ISBN 978-0-7369-6255-1 (eBook)
   1. Bible—Textbooks. 2. Boys—Religious life—Juvenile literature. I. Title.
   BS605.3.G47 2015
   220.6'1—dc23

                  2014035603

Printed in the United States of America

    15 16 17 18 19 20 21 22 23 / VP-CD / 10 9 8 7 6 5 4 3 2 1

For my awesome grandsons,

> Jacob Seitz
> Isaac Seitz
> Matthew Zaengle
> Ryan Zaengle

May you...

> Study the Bible to be wise;
> Believe it to be safe;
> Practice it to be holy.
> Study it through,
>
> > pray it in,
> > work it out,
> > note it down,
> > pass it on.[1]

Contents

The Bible Is...
the Greatest Book Ever Written

Did you know the Bible is the greatest book ever written? Well, it's true—and here are a few reasons why.

First, *the Bible claims to be written by God.* No other book in the whole world can make that claim. The Old Testament part of the Bible alone states more than 2000 times that it is the Word of God. And in the New Testament, the Bible is referred to as "the Word of God." The phrase "the Word of God" is used more than 40 times in the New Testament. When Jesus taught, *"the people were crowding around him and listening to the word of God"* (Luke 5:1).

And here's another reason the Bible is the greatest book ever written: *The Bible is indestructible.* Over the last 2000 years, there have been many attempts to destroy it, and it is still with us today. The Old and New Testaments have truly stood the test of time!

It's just like the Bible says about itself: *"The grass withers and the flowers fall, but the word of our God endures forever"* (Isaiah 50:8).

Why Is the Bible So Special?

That's the question you and I will be trying to answer in this book. Be ready to learn fascinating new things as you go on the amazing journey to discover how special the Bible is. Maybe you'll want to look at the Bible as an archaeologist would look at a rare and ancient artifact. Thinking and acting like an archaeologist, you would be very careful to inspect and analyze the Bible. You wouldn't want to miss any important clues about its origin and the information it contained, right?

Or maybe you could play the role of a master private investigator. Think of yourself as a young Sherlock Holmes! Having discovered this extremely unusual book, you would look through the Bible and search for clues that would reveal why it's so special.

Whether you see yourself as an archeologist or a private eye, this book you are holding in your hands—*A Boy's Guide to Understanding His Bible*—will be a key that helps you unlock the truth of why the Bible is the greatest book that's ever been written.

Fun in God's Word!

A great place to begin our journey is to see what the Bible says about itself. To do that you will need to have a pen or pencil handy and, of course, your Bible so you can write down some answers found in the Bible as we spell out B-I-B-L-E.

Bible reading is a must. I love summer vacation, don't you? One of my favorite summer activities as a boy was to go to the city pool as many times during the week as possible. I liked taking part in the many swim contests like seeing how fast I could swim back and forth across the pool.

And there was always a contest to see how far you could swim underwater on one breath! With practice I got pretty good at holding my breath. But eventually I had to come up for air. None of us can live without air.

Believe it or not, Bible reading should be as important to you as your need for air. How do these Bible writers describe the importance of reading the Bible? Or, what happens when you read God's Word, the Bible?

Like newborn babies, crave pure spiritual milk [the Bible], so that by it you may grow up in your salvation (1 Peter 2:2).

_____

_____

_____

I have treasured the words of His mouth [the Bible] more than my daily bread (Job 23:12).

_____

_____

_____

Think about it: How important is milk to a baby, and how necessary is physical food? The writers of these verses wanted you to know how important the Bible was to them. And now the question is, How important is the Bible to you? For the next seven days, circle each day you read your Bible:

Monday Tuesday Wednesday Thursday

Friday Saturday Sunday

Important decisions have their answers in the Bible.

What is the most important decision you have to make today, tomorrow, or this week? Jot it down here:

_____

At this time in your life, many decisions are being made for you by your parents and teachers. Maybe you don't even get to decide what to wear. Your mom is right there to make sure you don't wear the same T-shirt day after day.

But one day you will be making more and more of your own decisions. Does that scare you? Well, I have good news for you! The Bible has information and answers that can help you make those decisions.

Today, though, you get to decide each day how you act. You can be mean, or kind. You can be grumpy, or happy. You can lie, or tell the truth. You can be lazy, or helpful. What information does this verse tell you about your heart and its importance in making decisions??

Above all else, guard your heart, for everything you do flows from it (Proverbs 4:23).

You are to _____

Why? _____

_____

Bible truths give you direction. Have you ever been out hiking and sort of gotten lost? Or have you ever gotten lost or separated from your parents in the shopping mall? When you are sort of lost, you usually look for some landmark or building or familiar store that will help you figure out where you are. Well, the Bible and its truths are like that. They are your landmarks and signs, and they help you to know where you are.

In what direction do these Bible truths point you toward or away from?

My son, if sinful men entice you, do not give in to them (Proverbs 1:10).

God's truth tells you to _____

_____

_____

Do not be misled: "Bad company corrupts good character" (1 Corinthians 15:33).

God's truth tells you to _____

_____

Why? _____

_____

How can a young person stay on the path of purity? By living according to your word (Psalm 119:9).

God's truth tell you how to _____

_____

You are to _____

_____

Life changes come from the Bible. If you are like most guys your age, you can't wait to grow up. It seems like older boys get to do all the fun things like drive a car, stay up late, and play video games. Taking time to grow up is good and natural. You want—and need—to grow physically, which is a great change.

God also wants you to grow—to grow up spiritually, to grow and change to become more like Jesus. What do these verses say are some of the changes God wants for your life?

We...thank God...because your faith is growing more and more, and the love all of you have for one another is increasing (2 Thessalonians 1:3).

What two changes was the apostle Paul thankful for?

_____

_____

_____

_____

Grow in the grace and knowledge of our Lord and Savior Jesus Christ (2 Peter 3:18).

Peter told Jesus' followers to_____

_____

_____

Flee the evil desires of youth and pursue righteousness, faith, love and peace, along with those who call on the Lord out of a pure heart (2 Timothy 2:22).

What are you to flee from?_____

_____

What four things are you to pursue?

_____

_____

_____

_____

What kinds of friends should you have? _____

_____

_____

Eternal life is found in the Bible. When I was a young boy I found a book in the library about the globe-trotting adventures of the great Spanish explorer Juan Ponce de León. As legend has it, Ponce de León is said to have searched for the Fountain of Youth, which people believed could help restore a person's youth. You could say this is another way of searching for eternal life. Obviously Ponce de León didn't find the fountain because he has now been dead for almost 500 years. But Ponce de León did not have to travel halfway around the world to find eternal life.

What do these verses say you must do to have eternal life?

> God so loved the world that he gave his one and only Son, that whoever believes in him [Jesus] shall not perish but have eternal life (John 3:16).

_____

_____

> Whoever believes in the Son [Jesus] has eternal life, but whoever rejects the Son will not see life, for God's wrath remains on them (John 3:36).

A Boy's Guide to Discovering His Bible

What happens to those who believe in Jesus?

_____

What happens to those who don't believe in Jesus?

_____

_____

The wages of sin is death, but the gift of God is eternal life in Christ Jesus our Lord (Romans 6:23).

Regarding death: _____

_____

Regarding life: _____

_____

THE BIBLE IS...
the Greatest Book Ever Written

Do you have a favorite book? If so, how many times have you read it? I have a few favorite books too, and I've read them many times. They are entertaining, but not life-changing. But the Bible is very different from any other book you or I will ever read. It really can change lives.

So you can see why understanding the Bible is so important. If this is the greatest book ever written, then you need to know what God is saying to you. Unlike a favorite book that you may read for pleasure or enjoyment, your Bible will reveal something important and life-changing each time you open it. It is God's personal message to you, and in it He offers you the Words of Life.

★ Understanding Your Bible ★

This chapter helped you to learn some important things about the B-I-B-L-E. On this page, write out the point for each letter. (I'll get you started with "B.")

B ible reading is a must

I _____

B _____

L _____

E _____

Write out one thing you liked, learned, or want to do to better understand God's instructions to you in His Word, the Bible.

_____

_____

_____

The Bible Is...
a Book of Many Books

Have you thought much about how the Bible is organized, about the "big picture" of the Bible? Here's an exercise that will help you see how simple or basic the layout and structure of your Bible is. Once you get the big picture or overview of the Bible, you will be light years ahead of other people in the Bible study department.

So grab your Bible in hand, hold its spine in one hand, and fan through its pages with the other hand.

What did you notice? As the pages flew by, you probably saw that the Bible contains a bunch of different chapters in a lot of books. And you're right! The Bible is actually 66 different books, originally written in at least two languages (Hebrew and Greek), by more than 40 authors, and covering a period of at least 2000 years.

Many boys your age—and even many adults!— haven't thought much about how the Bible is organized. They don't understand how it all fits together. They also don't realize the relationship between the Old Testament and the New

Testament. And many times they decide that because one part of the Bible is called the New Testament, there's no reason to bother with reading and studying the Old Testament.

Well, get ready to discover how the different books of the Bible fit together. And don't worry or groan about what you think is coming. It's going to be fun—and it's going to be easy. You won't believe how much a few simple facts will help you understand the greatest book ever written!

To start, let's do a little survey of "the Book of many books." To do this you'll need to get your Bible and turn to the table of contents in the front. Follow along, and as you do, write your answers in the blank spaces on the upcoming pages.

A Big-Picture Survey of the Bible

The Old Testament

God founded the Hebrew nation to proclaim an important fact to a world that worshiped false gods: There is only one true, living God. The Old Testament is a record of God's dealings with His "chosen people," the Jewish people.

The first five books of the Old Testament—These books were written about 1449 BC (Before Christ) by God's servant Moses. They are called the Five Books of Moses, or the Pentateuch (meaning "five scrolls or writings" in the Greek language). In Judaism, they are called the Torah (meaning "law" in the Hebrew language). Using your Bible's table of contents, list the books below in the order you find them in your Bible. Also, notice the brief description of the contents of each of the books of the Bible.

1. _____ The book of beginnings (creation, man, sin, redemption, God's nation)

2. _____ God's deliverance of His people from Egypt

3. _____ Priestly laws on holiness and worship through sacrifices and purification

4. _____ Wanderings of God's people in the wilderness for 40 years due to disobedience

5. _____ Review of God's law by Moses to a new generation that will enter the Promised Land

The next 12 books of the Old Testament—These are the historical books. They were written about 1100–600 BC. They describe God's dealings with His chosen people after they entered the Promised Land—the land promised by God to Abraham and the people of Israel. List these 12 historical books in order and note the very brief explanation given about each book.

1. _____ Conquest of the Promised Land

2. _____ Disobedience and deliverance

3. _____ A story of a few faithful people during a dark time in Israel's history

4. _____ Transition from 12 tribes to a kingdom

5. _____ Coming together of the 12 tribes into the united kingdom of Israel

6. _____ A record of Israel dividing into two nations

7. _____ Details of the scattering of the northern and southern kingdoms of Israel

8. _____ A written record of Israel's spiritual history

9. _____ A written record of Israel's spiritual heritage

10._____ The people's return from captivity

11._____ Rebuilding of the wall around Jerusalem

12._____ Preservation of the Jewish people by Queen Esther

The next five books of the Old Testament—These are often referred to as the Wisdom Books. They are poetical and describe God's greatness and His dealings with mankind in Hebrew poetry and song. List these poetical books in order below and notice the theme of each book.

A Boy's Guide to Discovering His Bible

1. _____ The sufferings and loyal trust of a man who loved God

2. _____ A collection of 150 songs of praise and worship

3. _____ God's practical wisdom for successful living

4. _____ The emptiness of earthly life without God

5. _____ A portrait of God's love for His people

The next five books of the Old Testament—These are called the Major Prophets because of their length, not because they are more important. These books were written from about 750–550 BC. List them below and note the key theme of each book.

1. _____ Salvation through the coming Messiah

2. _____ Announcement of coming judgment

3. _____ A prophet's cry about the fall of Jerusalem

4. _____ An attempt to describe the glory of the Lord

5. _____ God is in control of all

The last 12 books of the Old Testament—These are called the Minor Prophets because they are generally shorter than the Major Prophets. These books were written from about 800–400 BC. List them in order and note the key theme of each book.

1. _____ Unfaithfulness of Israel

2. _____ The day of the Lord

3. _____ Judgment of Israel's northern kingdom

4. _____ The righteous judgment of Edom

5. _____ Demonstration of God's grace to the people in Nineveh

6. _____ Judgment of Israel's southern kingdom

7. _____ A warning that the city of Nineveh would be destroyed

8. _____ Importance of trusting God when things look bad

9. _____ The "great day of the Lord"

10._____ Details of the rebuilding of the temple

11._____ God's deliverance through the coming Messiah

12._____ Instruction against the outward keeping of a list of rules

Now do the math. Count how many books there are in the Old Testament and write your total here:

_____

Set a goal to memorize the names of these books and their order. You will never regret it. And you'll be able to quickly find every one of these books as you read and study your Bible.

The New Testament

The Old Testament provides a history of the preparation of the world for a great change. The law of Moses was meant to be a "tutor" to cause every person to realize the need for a Savior. In the New Testament we see God's ultimate goal fulfilled as He provides a Savior, the Messiah, Jesus Christ, who will rescue the world from sin. In the New Testament you will find:

—the life of Christ

—the beginning of Christianity

—the way of salvation

—instruction for Christian living and

—God's plan for the future

The first five books of the New Testament are *historical*. Look at your Bible's table of contents for the New Testament and list these five historical books in order below:

1. _____ The life of Christ—written especially for the Jewish people, revealing Jesus Christ as their long-awaited Messiah and King

2. _____ The life of Christ—revealing Jesus as the obedient Servant of God, emphasizing His daily activities

3. _____ The life of Christ—revealing Jesus as the perfect man, emphasizing His humanity

4. _____ The life of Christ—revealing Jesus as the Son of God, stressing His deity

5. _____ The beginning and spread of the Christian church—highlighting the ministry of the Holy Spirit

Just a note: The first four books above are referred to as the Four Gospels. Why four? Four different biographers recorded Jesus' life from four different perspectives: as a king, as a servant, as a man, and as God.

John 20:31 gives two results that come from studying the life of Jesus. List them here:

Result #1— _____

_____

Result #2— _____

_____

The next 21 books of the Bible are *letters*, or *epistles*. They were written to individuals, to churches, or to believers in general. These letters deal with every aspect of the Christian faith and every believer's responsibilities as a Christian. List these books of the Bible below in the same order as they appear in your Bible.

The apostle Paul's letters—written to churches or individuals.

1. _____ The righteousness of God

2. _____ Christian conduct

3. _____ The apostle Paul's defense of his apostleship

4. _____ Freedom in Christ

5. _____ Blessings in Christ

6. _____ The joy-filled life

7. _____ The supremacy of Christ

8. _____ Concern for the church

9. _____ Living in hope

10. _____ Instructions for a young disciple

11. _____ A charge to faithful ministry

12. _____ A manual of conduct

13. _____ Forgiveness

General letters—written to groups of Jewish people scattered throughout the Roman world.

14. _____ The superiority of Christ

15. _____ Genuine faith

16. _____ Responding to suffering

17. _____ Warning against false teachers

18. _____ Fellowship with God

19. _____ Christian wisdom and discernment

20. _____ Christian hospitality

21. _____ Defending faith in Christ

The last book of the New Testament is a book of *prophecy*. It tells of future events, including the return, reign, and glory of the Lord Jesus Christ, and describes the future for believers and unbelievers. This book of the Bible is named

_____

Add the number of books in both the New and Old Testaments to discover the total number of books in the Bible:

_____

These are the approved books that make up your Bible. Throughout time people have tried to add other books to this collection, but they were not approved by expert scholars in the early Christian church. The books you have in your Bible now are the authentic and complete Word of God.

Things to Remember from Your Journey Through the Bible

The focus of all the Bible is Christ. Even though Jesus was never mentioned by His name in the Old Testament, you can't miss the fact that He is the message of the entire Bible. What does Hebrews 1:2 say about Jesus' part in creating the universe?

> *In these last days he [God] has spoken to us by his Son, whom he appointed heir of all things, and through whom also he made the universe.*

_____

Isaiah the Prophet spoke of Jesus 700 years before His birth. In the verses below, circle the different facts we are told about Jesus coming to earth.

For unto us a Child is born,
Unto us a Son is given;
And the government will be upon His shoulder.
And His name will be called
Wonderful, Counselor, Mighty God,
Everlasting Father, Prince of Peace (Isaiah 9:6 NKJV).

Your salvation can be seen in both Old and New Testaments.
Read 2 Timothy 3:14-15 below and circle the different things
that helped Timothy understand salvation as he read and
studied what the Old Testament said about the coming Messiah, Christ Jesus.

But as for you [Timothy], continue in what you have learned
and have become convinced of, because you know those from
whom you learned it, and how from infancy you have known
the Holy Scriptures [the Old Testament], which are able to
make you wise for salvation through faith in Christ Jesus.

THE BIBLE IS...
a Book of Many Books

As you read through your Bible, imagine that you are
driving down a highway and reading the road signs. The first
sign gives you some information. Then the next sign gives
you more information. After you have passed all the signs,
you will have a complete understanding of what the creator
of those signs wanted you to know.

That's what will happen as you read and study your Bible.

A Boy's Guide to Discovering His Bible

As you go through the Old Testament, you will learn some information. Then as you read the New Testament you will get the complete picture and see how God's story is leading to the revelation of Jesus as the Savior of mankind.

But that's not all! The Bible tells you how to know Jesus and have a personal relationship with Him. It even shows you how to live your life God's way each and every day, in every situation. It truly has everything— creation, action, heroes, villains, a Savior, and instructions on how to live forever.

Wow—what a book!

The Bible Is...
a Book with a Spiritual Message

3

Do you ever have the feeling that something is missing in your life, but you're just not sure what? For instance, I remember going to church each week as a boy about your age. Sure, I went with my parents every Sunday. It was what our family did every week, and I didn't give them any trouble about attending church.

But once I got there, I was miserable. I sat there wondering, *So what's the big deal about church? I don't get it. In fact, I think church is boring. Well, except I do get to see some of my friends when I'm there. That's cool.*

Every week, Sunday school seemed pretty much the same. Each Sunday, the teacher would tell us, "Be sure you read your Bible every day."

Oh yeah, the Bible. I didn't get that either. Every time I tried to read the Bible at home—the one my parents had given me—or every time I sat in church and listened (well, sort of) to a sermon or someone teaching from the Bible, I was totally confused. I couldn't get why the things in the Bible were so important.

And it wasn't because I lacked mental ability. I made pretty good grades in school, and if I had really wanted to, I probably could have made straight A's every term. But when it came to the Bible and spiritual things, it was as if I needed some serious help in order to understand what I was hearing and reading.

Has that been your experience too? Can you relate? Have you been there and done that—maybe even every Sunday?

Fun in God's Word!

If some of what I just described fits your situation, you will like this chapter. We're going to see what it means to read and study the Bible through "spiritual eyes." The Bible is a spiritual book, written and preserved by God for His people. That means you need spiritual help to understand it, to get it. And that, my friend, brings us to this chapter about the Holy Spirit. As a part of the Godhead—the "trinity" made up of God the Father, Jesus the Son, and the Holy Spirit—one of the Holy Spirit's roles is helping you understand the Bible.

Once again, have a pen or pencil handy and, of course, your Bible, so that you can write down some answers as we spell out S-P-I-R-I-T.

Spiritual understanding comes from the Holy Spirit. Open your Bible to 1 Corinthians 2:14, or follow along by reading the words below. This verse explains the role the Holy Spirit has when it comes to helping us understanding the Bible:

*The person without the Spirit does **not accept** the things that come from the Spirit of God, but considers them foolishness, and **cannot understand them**, because they are discerned [understood] only through the Spirit.*

What two responses does a person without the Holy Spirit have when he reads God's Word? (See bold words for a hint.)

Response #1 _____

_____

Response #2 _____

_____

Possessing the Spirit. I'm sure you can see how important it is to have God's Spirit helping you when you read and study the Bible. So the obvious question is, How can someone have or possess God's Spirit? To answer this question, read Acts 2:38 below. What gift does God give each person who turns away from sin to believe in Jesus and follow Him?

Each of you must repent of your sins and turn to God, and be baptized in the name of Jesus Christ for the forgiveness of your sins. Then you will receive the gift of the Holy Spirit (NLT).

_____

Just a note: Repent means saying—and meaning—you are truly sorry for doing anything that does not please God, and asking Jesus to come into your life and help you do what is right. When you mean this sincerely with all your heart, you receive Jesus' Spirit, the Holy Spirit. He actually comes to live inside you and be your helper! How neat is that?

Have you asked Jesus into your life? You can do that right now and have Jesus' Spirit live in your heart. Here's a prayer that might help give words to your heart's desire:

A Prayer to Pray

God, I want to be Your child, a true boy after Your heart. I want to live my life in You and for You, and not for myself. I admit that I am a sinner and often fail to do what You say is right. I receive Your Son, Jesus Christ, into my heart. Thank You that He died on the cross for my sins. Thank You for giving me Your grace and Your strength so that I can follow You with all my heart. Amen.

If you have made this decision, tell your parents or your Sunday school teacher. They will be so happy that you have decided to follow Jesus.

Instruction comes from the Holy Spirit. Who is your favorite teacher in school? I bet you enjoy that person's teaching and look forward to that class. But what about having the Holy Spirit as your teacher? What two learning aids does the Holy Spirit provide for you, according to John 14:26?

> *The Advocate, the Holy Spirit, whom the Father will send in my name, will teach you all things and will remind you of everything I have said to you.*

1. _____

_____

2. _____

_____

Resist the habit of not asking for help. Now let's look at a different version of John 14:26. What is the Spirit called?

> *The Helper, the Holy Spirit, whom the Father will send in My name, He will teach you all things, and bring to your remembrance all things that I said to you* (NKJV).

_____

In the verse below, what did Jesus say He would do after He returned to heaven?

I will pray the Father, and He will give you another Helper, that He may abide with you forever" (John 14:16 NKJV).

_____

_____

Jesus promised to send another Helper, the Holy Spirit. This Helper is ready to assist you, just as Jesus would help if He were physically standing next to you. So why wouldn't you want to talk to Jesus' Helper and ask for His help? That's a no-brainer!

What does the Bible say will happen when you pray and call out to God?

Call to me and I will answer you (Jeremiah 33:3).

_____

But what if you don't know how to ask for help, or you don't know what kind of help you need? With pen in hand, how does the Bible say the Spirit helps even when you don't know how to pray and ask for help?

In the same way, the Spirit helps us in our weakness. We do not know what we ought to pray for, but the Spirit himself intercedes for us (Romans 8:26).

_____

_____

Insures you behave like Jesus. Besides helping you understand your Bible, the Holy Spirit gives you the help you need to act the right way—God's way. The Spirit's power will help you walk by the Spirit and display His "fruit of the Spirit." Read Galatians 5:22-23 and underline each fruit (or attitude) God wants on display in your life.

> *The fruit of the Spirit is love, joy, peace, forbearance, kindness, goodness, faithfulness, gentleness and self-control.*

You know what love, joy, and peace are, but what about "forbearance"? Look up this word in a dictionary and write the definition here:

_____

_____

_____

Kindness—This is the opposite of being mean. You know when you are being mean to your little sister or another kid at school. Ask God to help you find ways to be nice and do kind things toward others, starting at home with your parents and brothers and sisters.

Goodness—This means not doing bad things like lying, stealing, or cheating on tests at school. Sometimes it's hard to do what is right, but you have help! God's Spirit will enable you to do what is good.

Faithfulness—To be faithful means you will always do what you say you'll do. You will keep your promises.

When you ask God's Spirit to help you be faithful, then people will know they can count on you to do what you say you'll do.

Gentleness—This means you are not rough or harsh in the way you act toward people. Again, the Holy Spirit is available to help you be gentle.

Self-control—This means controlling your emotions. With the help of the Holy Spirit's power, you can say no to outbursts or fits of anger. You can make the choice to not do anything rash. You will be able to say no to things you know are not right. You will gladly listen to the rules set by your parents and other people in authority.

The actions, behaviors, and attitudes that make up the fruit of the Spirit are expressions of Jesus' life and character produced in you by His Spirit. When you "walk by the Spirit" and obey God in all you do, what will be the result, according to Galatians 5:16?

Walk by the Spirit, and you will not gratify the desires of the flesh.

The result? _____

_____

In simple terms, to "walk by the Spirit" means obeying God's Word. Instead of wanting to do bad things, or lie, or yell in anger, or sulk and pout, when you walk by Jesus' Spirit, you will want to do what is right.

Trust the Spirit as a guide. You know what a guide does—he helps you find your way. He keeps you from getting lost or hurt. What does Jesus promise the Spirit will do for you?

> *When he, the Spirit of truth, comes, he will guide you into all the truth* (John 16:13).

_____

_____

The Holy Spirit is the absolute best guide you could have! Why? Because when He leads you, you will know the right things to do. As the verse above says, "He will guide you into all the truth." When you allow God's Spirit to lead you, you are showing proof of your relationship with God. When you are being "led by the Spirit of God," what does it prove?

> *Those who are led by the Spirit of God are the children of God* (Romans 8:14).

_____

What a great God you have! As a child of God, you have the Holy Spirit living in you. The Spirit can guide you in the right ways to go, even when you aren't sure of what you should do. The Spirit's role in your life guides you to the truth—to do the right thing.

THE BIBLE IS...
a Book with a Spiritual Message

You are just beginning your journey toward understanding the Bible better. And probably one of the most amazing things about the Bible is that God Himself speaks to you through His Word. But because God's message is spiritual, you need help to understand it. That's where the Holy Spirit comes to the rescue! He is your very own teacher and tutor—He can help you understand God's Word and to know the answers you have to life's important questions. He wants to—and can—help you unlock the secrets of the Bible.

Truly understanding the Bible begins when you become a Christian and receive the gift of the Holy Spirit. You don't become a Christian just by going to church or raising your hand at a Christian camp. Being a Christian means receiving Jesus into your life and following Him.

When you turn your life over to Jesus, His Spirit comes to live in you, to help and guide you in all that you say, think, and do. And, as you know by now, He helps you to understand your Bible!

★ Understanding Your Bible ★

In this chapter you looked at the Person who can help you understand your Bible, the S-P-I-R-I-T. To assist you in remembering some of the points from this chapter, write out the point of each letter. (I'll get you started with "S.")

A Boy's Guide to Discovering His Bible

Spiritual understanding comes from the Holy Spirit

P _____

I _____

R _____

I _____

T _____

Write out one thing you liked, learned, or want to do to better understand God's instructions to you in His Word, the Bible.

_____

_____

_____

_____

The Bible Is...
a Book Filled with Fantastic True Stories

4

I f I asked you what two classes you dislike most in school, you might say, "English grammar and English literature." Maybe that's why many boys of all ages can't or won't read the Bible—because the Bible is grammatically constructed and it is literature.

As you begin the journey toward understanding your Bible, it helps to know that the Bible is made up of several different types of literature. It contains poetry, prophecy, teaching, and narrative (or, as your English teacher would call it, prose).

Narratives are stories, and in the Bible you find God's story—a story that is utterly true and very important. Bible narratives tell you about things that happened in the past, stories about certain people and, most of all, about God.

The purpose of the stories in the Bible is to show God at work in His creation and among His people. The narrative books of the Bible honor God and help you to understand and appreciate Him. These stories give you a picture of God's care and protection of His followers. They also provide many important lessons for you about your life.

Fun in God's Word!

You now know that Genesis is the first book in the Bible. Genesis is a narrative, a story. Read the story in Genesis 1:1-5 below, then answer a few questions:

1 *In the beginning God created the heavens and the earth.*

2 *Now the earth was formless and empty, darkness was over the surface of the deep, and the Spirit of God was hovering over the waters.*

3 *And God said, "Let there be light," and there was light.*

4 *God saw that the light was good, and he separated the light from the darkness.*

5 *God called the light "day," and the darkness he called "night." And there was evening, and there was morning—the first day.*

What is this story about?

_____

_____

_____

A Boy's Guide to Discovering His Bible

What does this story tell you about God?

_____

_____

_____

What answers do these verses give about the origin of the world—about the creation of the world and all that is in it?

_____

_____

_____

All narratives have a storyline or plot. They also have characters, whether spiritual beings (like angels), humans, or animals. In the Old Testament part of the Bible, the stories have plots that are part of God's special plan for the world. These stories also have a special cast of characters, the most special character of all being God Himself!

To follow up on your reading from Genesis 1 take a moment now to read Genesis 3:1-7:

> 1 *Now the serpent was more crafty than any of the wild animals the* LORD *God had made. He said to the woman, "Did God really say, 'You must not eat from any tree in the garden'?"*
>
> 2 *The woman said to the serpent, "We may eat fruit from the trees in the garden,*

3 *but God did say, 'You must not eat fruit from the tree that is in the middle of the garden, and you must not touch it, or you will die.'"*

4 *"You will not certainly die," the serpent said to the woman.*

5 *"For God knows that when you eat from it your eyes will be opened, and you will be like God, knowing good and evil."*

6 *When the woman saw that the fruit of the tree was good for food and pleasing to the eye, and also desirable for gaining wisdom, she took some and ate it. She also gave some to her husband, who was with her, and he ate it.*

7 *Then the eyes of both of them were opened, and they realized they were naked; so they sewed fig leaves together and made coverings for themselves.*

Who are the characters in this story?

_____

_____

_____

What is the story line, or what is the plot? Or, what's happening here?

_____

_____

_____

What was the result of the man and woman's actions?

_____

_____

_____

Based on reading these verses, how would you answer someone who asked you, "Where did sin come from?"

_____

_____

_____

Congratulations! You have successfully completed the first step toward understanding your Bible. *What did I do?* you wonder. You simply read a portion of the Bible—in this case, seven verses—and noticed a few key things. And look at how much you learned!

Now let's spell out R-E-A-D-I-N-G because this is Step #1 toward understanding your Bible. You need to learn how to read the Bible.

Even though the Bible is like any other book with black ink on white paper, it is also very special. It's extra special because it's God's message to you, and you don't want to miss anything He is saying to you. Here are some general guidelines to keep in mind as you read your Bible.

Realize the Bible is like any other book. This is true when it comes to reading and studying the Bible. Would God hide the meaning of the verses you are reading? Do you need special glasses to read God's true message somewhere between the lines? You know the answers: Of course not!

God wrote the Bible just like every author who writes a book. He had one message in mind when He wrote it, whether to those who were reading it thousands of years ago or to those like you who are alive and reading it today. Your mission is to find out what the Bible's message means and then apply it to your life today.

Enlist the help of a Bible you can understand. Over the many years since the Bible was written, it has been made available in different versions. Today there are many versions available. Ask your parents to help you pick one that is clearest to you so that you understand what you are reading.

Always look for the "big picture." If you have a study Bible, read the notes and comments that are on the pages you are studying. Also read the introduction to the book of the Bible you are reading. Knowing more about the big picture and what's happening will help you understand what the author of the verse or passage of the Bible was thinking and what he wants you to know.

Dictionaries can help you with difficult words. How do you build your vocabulary as you read books at school or for fun? You look in a dictionary for the meanings of the words you don't know, right? You can do the same when you are reading the Bible.

Investigate what you are reading. As you are reading in your Bible, remember to ask yourself, "What is this paragraph about? Does what I'm reading apply to me? If so, how?" As you do this paragraph after paragraph, you will begin to see what each paragraph is about as well as figure out the meaning of the entire passage.

Never speed-read the Bible. Your goal is not to see how fast you can read your Bible or Sunday school lesson. Rather, take time to understand and remember what you read. Read your Bible with the goal of letting God change your life. Read it for wisdom and encouragement. Read so that tomorrow or maybe even in a year from now you will remember what you read today.

Grab a pen or pencil as you read. Don't be afraid to underline passages or circle words that stand out as you read. The Bible is just physical ink and paper. It's not the physical book that is sacred—it's God's message within the book that is sacred. And God wants you to understand your Bible. So go ahead and mark it! Underline and circle key words or phrases. Write short notes in the margins. All your markings with a pen or pencil will help you to better remember God's message to you.

The Story of David and Goliath

By now you've had some practice reading Bible passages. Now let's do it for real. Let's look at every young man's favorite Bible hero, David. Begin by reading 1 Samuel 17:19-58 in your Bible. Don't be afraid to mark or circle key words or phrases as you read. After you have read the passage, put a check mark here and answer the questions that follow:

_____

Look again at verses 19-23. What is said about these main characters?

Saul—

_____

_____

_____

David—

_____

_____

_____

David's brothers (hint: see 1 Samuel 16:10)—

_____

_____

Goliath—

_____

_____

How did the soldiers of Israel respond to Goliath's presence (verse 24)?

_____

_____

How did David's older brother respond to David's presence in the camp (verse 28)?

_____

_____

Even though everyone else was afraid, what did David say he would do (verse 32)?

_____

_____

King Saul wanted David to wear armor to fight Goliath. But what was David's choice of weapons (verse 40)?

_____

_____

_____

Goliath was fighting for the Philistines. Who did David say he was fighting for (verse 45)?

_____

_____

_____

What was the result of the battle between David and Goliath (verses 49-50)?

_____

_____

_____

What does this story teach you about trusting God when you have a problem?

_____

_____

_____

Why do you think David refused to respond to being ridiculed and bullied by his oldest brother, or by Saul calling him a "kid," or by Goliath's taunts? (Hint: See verses 37 and 45.)

_____

_____

_____

Based on how David responded to his problems, how can you respond when problems arise at home or school?

_____

_____

_____

THE BIBLE IS...
a Book Filled with Fantastic True Stories

Maybe you have wished life were easier. All you want to do is have some fun, maybe play a few video games, watch some TV, or play baseball or kick a soccer ball with your friends. But your parents make you go to school and sit in a classroom and do stuff you don't like or is boring. But because of what you are learning in school, you are growing mentally at the same time you are growing physically. And just think—in just a few years, you will be driving a car!

In the same way that you are growing mentally and physically, you also want to be growing spiritually. To do that, you need to read the Bible. And you can use the skills you are learning in this book—skills that will help you understand your Bible and learn God's message to you.

What is God's message? Consider what you learned from the story about David. He was brave. He stood up for what he believed. His faith in God gave him the ability to stand up and do what was right.

Now think about your own life. Doesn't David's courage give you even a little bit of courage to live more for God each day? Doesn't his bold faith in God help you to trust God more? That's God's message to you, and it is just one of the hundreds of stories from God's book waiting for you to read, enjoy, and make a part of your own life. As the Bible says,

This God is our God for ever and ever; he will be our guide even to the end (Psalm 48:14).

The God David trusted in is the same God you can trust in—through every day and every trial.

★ Understanding Your Bible ★

In this chapter you learned that the Bible is a book of stories. Reading unlocks these stories so you can apply their lessons to your own life. So, R-E-A-D-I-N-G your Bible is an important first step toward spiritual growth. Write out the point of each letter. (I'll get you started with "R.")

Realize the Bible is like other books

E_____

A_____

D_____

I_____

N_____

G_____

Write out one thing you liked, learned, or want to do to better understand God's instructions to you in His Word, the Bible.

_____

_____

The Best Kind of Studying

If you're a Christian, it makes sense that you'd want to learn as much as you could about Jesus Christ and his Word. You can do that by talking about the Bible with your friends and family, writing down verses or memorizing them. You can also learn by going to church and listening to what your pastor or youth leader says.

Think about it—of all the things you learn in your life, what's the most important? It's not algebra or biology! Although studying these subjects is important and necessary, the most important thing is to know who God is and what he wants you to do in your life. And the more you learn about him, the more you feel secure and have strength for whatever challenges you have to face. Reading the Bible is the best kind of studying![2]

—Kelli

The Bible Is...
a Book to Be Observed

5

"It's a bird...It's a plane...No, it's Superman!" These statements are familiar to you if you are a fan of the Superman comics, cartoons, or action movie series. There is even a TV series about Superman as a boy and teenager.

However, this chapter isn't about a comic book hero. But it *is* about looking. In the Superman comics, when people looked up, some thought they saw a bird in flight. Others thought they saw an airplane. Still others saw who it really was—Superman! In this chapter about understanding your Bible, we are going to learn about how to look and see what the Bible actually says. We are going to learn how to *really* look!

Have you ever played a game in which one person silently acts something out, and other people have to guess what is being acted out? The person doing the acting cannot say anything, but will use his or her face, hands, and body to give clues. Sometimes he or she will move around a lot or even act crazy. And those who are watching have to guess the correct answer for what's being acted out.

During such a game, those who are watching will give all sorts of answers. Many times they won't agree on what they are seeing. Why is that? A lot of times it is because they aren't all paying careful attention to what the "actor" is doing. They aren't looking closely at what they are seeing.

When it comes to looking at the world around us, many times we don't pay careful attention to what is happening. We don't notice the specifics. We are guilty of what Jesus said about some people: *"You have eyes but fail to see"* (Mark 8:18).

It's the same problem that comes up when several people witness an accident. They all see it differently, and sometimes they don't see every detail correctly. So when the police ask the eyewitnesses what they saw, they get several different views of the accident. That makes it hard for the officers to figure out what really happened.

That's why good observation skills are so important. When it comes to reading the Bible, how do you become a better observer? Like those who work for the police, FBI, CIA, or any other law enforcement agency, you have to be trained to look for specifics—you have to have a good eye for details.

Fun in God's Word!

In the last chapter you discovered the first step for gaining a better understanding of your Bible. What acrostic did we use to describe that first step? (If you need to, you can look in the previous chapter to find the answer.)

____-____-____-____-____-____-____

Now for Step #2! As you begin to develop a better understanding of your Bible you must learn to look more closely at what you are reading. This step is called *observation*. It requires being more careful as you look at and read the Bible. Get a pen or pencil and, of course, your Bible so you can write down some answers as you learn what it means to O-B-S-E-R-V-E.

Observation requires focus. Most of your day is spent with your family at home, with kids at school, and with other people in various activities. All day long, you are involved with a lot of different people and activities.

Because you are involved with so many different people and activities, you don't have much opportunity to focus on just one thing. But when it comes to reading your Bible, it's important that you focus on it with your full attention. The Bible is important, so when you read it, you need to set aside a quiet time that allows you to focus on what it is saying. Reading your Bible is like listening to your parents. They want your complete, undivided attention. And—you guessed it— God wants your full attention too. Even more so!

So when you read your Bible, learn to focus. Don't let the sights and sounds that fill your day crowd out your time with God. According to Psalm 119:15, how did the psalmist describe his desire to focus on God's Word? As always, use your pen or pencil to fill in the blanks.

I meditate on your precepts and consider your ways.

— I _____ on your precepts

— and _____ your ways.

Just a note: The word *meditate* means to think about something for a while. The word *consider* means to give something your continued, undivided attention. God wants to speak to you, and He does not want you to be distracted.

Be aware of words. There are many words that can have several different meanings. For example, consider the word *trunk*. It can mean several different things. How many meanings does the word *trunk* have? Write as many of these meanings as you can think of. I'll start by giving you one example:

Tree trunk

_____

_____

_____

Now, write as many meanings as you can think of for the word *coast*.

_____

When a word becomes part of a group of words in a sentence, then its specific meaning becomes clearer. For example, in the sentence "The oak tree has a big trunk," the word *trunk* can have only one possible meaning. If you don't know the meaning of a word you see in your Bible, look it up in a dictionary. Just make sure the definition in the dictionary fits with how the word is used in the sentence you are looking at.

Structure is crucial. When you read or write, a line of words that ends with a period is called a sentence. When sentences are put together as a group, they are called a paragraph. In a book, there are two, three, or more paragraphs on each page, and each paragraph is usually a complete thought.

Imagine an author is writing about the variety of fish that live in the ocean. He would write about sea turtles in one paragraph, and he would write about swordfish in another paragraph because they are not the same kind of sea animal. After he writes a paragraph describing sea turtles, he would then begin a new paragraph to describe swordfish. Whenever an author begins a new paragraph, it is a clue to you that he might be switching subjects (like in our example—switching from sea turtles to swordfish).

Paragraphs are separated by a short "indent" on the first line of a new paragraph. Each time you arrive at a new paragraph, the first line is shorter than the rest of the lines in that same paragraph. An indented line is a clue that tells you the author is switching to a new point or subject.

Read Mark 1:29-34, and observe what happens as you go from one paragraph to the next.

What is the subject of the paragraph in Mark 1:29-31?

_____

_____

_____

(Notice the line spacing or indent between this paragraph and the next.)

What is the subject of the paragraph in Mark 1:32-34?

_____

_____

_____

Emphasis means something. If you have something *really* important to say, and you want to make sure your parents or your friends hear what you say, what do you do? You may start by saying, "Please listen. This is important!" or "You're not going to believe this!" You state your big news in a way that causes others to listen. We see this in the Bible as well.

For example, how did Moses begin Deuteronomy 6:4 to make sure his listeners knew that what he was about to say was important? Or put another way, how did Moses get their attention?

Hear, O Israel: The LORD our God, the LORD is one.

_____

_____

In the New Testament, the apostle Paul also needed to get the attention of his audience. He is about to spend time writing three chapters(!) about how important the Jewish people are to God, and he wants to make sure his readers get the message. Look at Romans 9:1 and write out the words Paul used to get people's attention.

I speak the truth in Christ—I am not lying, my conscience confirms it through the Holy Spirit...

Claim #1—_____

_____

Claim #2—_____

_____

Claim #3—_____

_____

Repeated information is important. If you have something important to say, what can you do to make sure one of your buddies gets the point? You can repeat what's important, right? The Bible does this. For example:

What word does Jesus repeat at the beginning of each verse in Matthew 5:3-10?

_____

In Matthew 5:3-10, Jesus wants to make it clear how people will feel if they act in a godly way. *Just a note:* In these verses, the word "blessed" means "happy."

How many times are the words "love" or "it" mentioned in 1 Corinthians 13:4-8?_____

Value asking questions. Looking carefully at what you are reading in the Bible requires that you ask the right questions. A journalist is a reporter who gathers facts and information for news reports or newspaper articles. When you get to high school, you might have the opportunity to enroll in a journalism class. Your teacher might even send you "into the field" to report on an event at your school or in the local area. As you do the research that will help you create your report, you would ask certain kinds of questions, called WH questions. These questions are:

Who?

Where?

When?

What?

Why?

Using the WH questions, read Mark 1:29-31 again in your Bible and practice observing:

Question #1: *Who?* Who are the people in this paragraph? Note them all.

_____

_____

What is said about each of these people?

_____

_____

_____

Question #2: *Where?* Where is this taking place? Note all descriptive information.

_____

_____

_____

Question #3: *When?* When is this taking place? Note all mentions of time.

_____

_____

_____

Question #4: *What?* What is taking place in this paragraph? What's happening?

_____

_____

_____

Question #5: *Why?* Why do you think God wanted this information in the Bible? What did God want everyone to know?

_____

_____

_____

Examine the kinds of literature. The Bible is a book made up of more than one kind of literature. We have already looked at the parts of the Bible that tell a story, called narrative or prose. Here are the other types of literature you will find in your Bible:

Discourse—When the material you are reading in your Bible is made up of teaching, it is called discourse—which means a discussion on a subject. For instance, when your teachers at school teach on a subject, they are using discourse. In the Bible, a discourse is usually given in a formal presentation with a topic in mind. Look again at Deuteronomy 6:5-9. What was the subject of Moses' teaching? (Hint: Commandments are God's laws.)

_____

_____

_____

Poetry—Much of the poetry in the Bible is found in the books of Psalms, Proverbs, and Song of Songs (or Song of Solomon).

Look at the book of Proverbs. How many chapters are in the book of Proverbs? _____

Read Proverbs 1:8-9. What advice is given to you as a young man?

_____

_____

Look at the book of Psalms. How many chapters are in this book? _____

Parables—The portions of the Bible that use stories to communicate a specific truth are called parables. Look at Matthew 13 in your Bible for some examples of Jesus' parables.

Prophecy—The sections of the Bible that deal with future events are called prophecies. For example, back in the Old Testament, we find prophecies that talk about the birth of Jesus. These prophecies were given hundreds of years before Jesus was born! Prophecies talk about things that haven't happened yet.

THE BIBLE IS...
a Book to Be Observed

When it comes to understanding the Bible, more is involved than just a casual reading of the words. It requires taking time to understand what is being said. If you want to get more out of your Bible, then it's important to become a good observer. The skill of observation can be learned, developed, and improved. Just as a police detective is trained in how and what to observe, you can learn what to look for as you read your Bible. Best of all, with this knowledge comes understanding, which helps you know what God is asking of you.

★ Understanding Your Bible ★

In this chapter you learned to carefully observe what is written in your Bible. It's as if you were looking at your Bible under a microscope. So to O-B-S-E-R-V-E your Bible you are using the microscope of asking questions that help you to understand the text. To help you remember the key lessons in this chapter, write out the point of each letter. (I'll get you started with "O.")

Observation requires concentration

B_____

S_____

E_____

R_____

V_____

E_____

Write out one thing you liked, learned, or want to do to better understand God's instructions to you in His Word, the Bible.

_____

_____

The Bible Is...
a Book You Can Understand

6

Suppose a friend or even a stranger came up to you and handed you a note that read,

The extent of something is in direct proportion to the sum of nothing divided by its separate parts.

If you're like me, you would give the note a blank stare because you would have no idea what it is saying. There is no clear message in the note.

Or how about receiving a note that says, "Alabby labbakayon Justinabokin."

Once again, there is no clear message. Why? Because these are just random letters on a piece of paper.

Unfortunately, many guys your age regard the Bible as they would regard these two notes. The popular thinking goes like this: "The Bible is supposedly a message from God written with words we can recognize, but whose meaning is mostly unclear and way beyond our understanding."

That's why there are some people who believe you need

an expert to explain God's message to you. You know, someone like your parents or a Sunday school teacher. Or maybe you believe you must wait until you're older before you can really understand the meaning of what you read in your Bible. Well, hang on, my friend. You are about to discover that you *can* understand your Bible...and that it's actually fun!

Fun in God's Word!

I hope you are realizing the Bible isn't such a mysterious book or that only a select few can understand it. No, the Bible can be understood by guys your age as well.

So far, you have looked at two steps in the process toward understanding your Bible—

Step #1—READ your Bible.

Step #2—OBSERVE closely what you are reading.

Now you are ready for the next step:

Step #3—UNDERSTAND your Bible by drawing conclusions about what a verse or passage means.

By now you know the drill. Go get a pencil or pen, and of course, your Bible, so you can write down some answers as we look at God's Word and spell out M-E-A-N-I-N-G.

Meanings are always "plain" or obvious. What do I mean by "plain" meaning? I could use the word *simple* or *natural*. For instance, have you ever read classic boys' books like *Treasure Island* or *Two Years Before the Mast*? In these books there are no transformers or superheroes. They are adventure books about real live boys, plain and simple. These books are understood by the plain and natural meaning of their contents. There are no hidden messages or mysterious meanings.

That is true about the Bible as well. When you read it, you are to look for the natural, plain meaning of the text. You don't need to look for some deep, secret meaning hidden within the verses you are reading. God wrote the Bible so you could understand its message. He doesn't want to leave you guessing. He wants His words to be plain and obvious.

One reason the plain meaning is important is so you can avoid people who try to tell you something that the Bible doesn't say. For example, some people claim they know the time and day when Jesus will return to earth. But what did Jesus say in Mark 13:32? What is the plain meaning of His words?

> About that day or hour no one knows, not even the angels in heaven.

There is no hidden meaning in this verse. Jesus said no one can predict when He will return. So do not listen to anyone who claims to know when He will come back.

Examine the author's reason for writing. As you read your Bible, it's easy to make the mistake of assuming that your present-day understanding of what you are reading is the same as what the author was trying to say. Remember, the Bible was written thousands of years ago. So it's important to know what the author was trying to say so that you understand your Bible correctly.

For consider the word "cross" in Matthew 16:24. What do you think Jesus meant by the following statement?

Whoever wants to be my disciple must deny themselves and take up their cross and follow me.

_____

_____

When you think of a cross, you are probably thinking about a piece of jewelry that your sister or mom wears on a chain around their neck. But is that what Jesus' listeners would have understood when they heard Jesus say these words 2000 years ago?

In the first century, during the time of Jesus, the cross was an instrument of shame. Criminals or runaway slaves were put to death on wood crosses—that is, crosses were used for torture and death.

Going back to what Jesus said: What would Jesus' listeners be thinking of when He said that a person "must deny himself and take up his cross"? They would have realized that following Jesus meant being willing to be rejected by others and maybe even dying a horrible death on a cross. Following Jesus would have required a serious commitment!

Write out a brief statement about your commitment to following Jesus and any changes you may need to make.

_____

_____

All of the Bible is useful. God's Word has eternal value— it speaks to all people, for all times, in all cultures, and has the authority of God behind every word of it. The words God spoke in the past were directed toward the people who were alive at that time, but we who are alive today can still learn valuable lessons from them. What four things is the Bible useful for, according to the verse below?

All Scripture is God-breathed and is useful for teaching, rebuking, correcting and training in righteousness (2 Timothy 3:16).

1._____

2._____

3._____

4._____

Remember, just because parts of God's Word were directed to people in the past doesn't mean those parts are useless to you. All of the Bible is useful! You just need to understand what it says, and how to apply the lessons to your own life.

Note the "three Cs." Your goal in Bible study is to determine the plain meaning of what you are reading. Here are three helpful *C* questions you can ask along with your WH questions (Who, What, Where, When, Why).

C Question #1: What is the CONTEXT?—*Context* refers to the Bible text that precedes or follows a specific word or passage in the Bible. Context usually influences the meaning of the written text.

For example, read Mark 1:29-31 and list the people in this passage:

> 29 *As soon as they left the synagogue, they went with James and John to the home of Simon and Andrew.*
>
> 30 *Simon's mother-in-law was in bed with a fever, and they immediately told Jesus about her.*
>
> 31 *So he went to her, took her hand and helped her up. The fever left her and she began to wait on them.*

_____

_____

_____

To discover the *context* of Mark 1:29-31, read Mark 1:21-28. *Where* did the events of Mark 1:29-31 take place, according to verse 21?

_____

What day of the week did the events of Mark 1:29-31 take place, according to verse 21?

_____

Now you know exactly what was happening immediately before the events described in Mark 1:29-31. This is *context*. It's been said that 75 percent of your questions about a specific passage can be answered by looking at the verses just before or just after the passage you are studying. So don't forget to note CONTEXT.

C Question #2: Are there CROSS-REFERENCES you can study?—Cross-references are other verses that use the same words or convey the same meaning as the verse you are reading. If you are having trouble understanding a verse, you can check other similar verses in the Bible for help.

For example, the WH question "Who was Simon?" is not fully answered in Mark 1:29-31, nor is it found in the context of Mark 1:16-20. But if you look at Matthew 4:18, a cross-reference, you will find your answer along with other information about Simon's job and how Jesus met him.

As Jesus was walking beside the Sea of Galilee, he saw two brothers, Simon called Peter and his brother Andrew. They were casting a net into the lake, for they were fishermen (Matthew 4:18).

Who was Simon?

_____

What was his profession?

_____

What was his brother's name?

_____

Where did these two brothers work?

_____

C Question #3: What was the CULTURE like when these words were written?—*Culture* has to do with the way people lived at a certain time in history and is influenced by the location where they lived. The Bible is an ancient book written thousands of years ago in a Middle Eastern culture. Look at the maps in your Bible, or in an atlas, or on the Internet, and find where the Middle East is located. When you've done this, place a check mark here. _____

Middle Eastern culture has not changed much in 2000 years. Many of the people who live there today still ride camels and herd sheep. This has long been part of their culture. However, many of us do not know much about Middle Eastern culture and customs. For that reason, when we want to discover the meaning of a verse, we must learn more about the places where the Bible was written and the time period during which it was written. This background information can help us understand the Bible better.

What custom do you see described below?

Jesus...got up from the meal, took off his outer clothing, and wrapped a towel around his waist. After that, he poured water into a basin and began to wash his disciples' feet, drying them with the towel that was wrapped around him (John 13:3-5).

_____

_____

Israel was (and still is) a dry and dusty land. In Jesus' day, it was the custom for people to wash the feet of their visitors. The person who carried out this task was usually a lowly servant. But in John 13:3-5, no servant was available, and none of the disciples were willing to perform this service. Who ended up washing the 12 disciples' filthy feet (including Judas's)?

_____

Thinking of Jesus—God in human flesh—and His example of being a humble servant, what will you do the next time you are asked to take out the trash or make your bed, or the next time you see someone who could use a helping hand?

_____

_____

Interpret what you know. Who would you look to for help if someone were to come up to you and speak in a language you don't understand? You would need an interpreter, right? You would need someone who can explain to you what that person is saying.

An interpreter is also helpful for when you study the Bible. And, believe it or not, with what you have learned so far, you are well on your way to becoming an interpreter of what God says in His Word.

Jesus, the greatest interpreter and master of explaining God's Word, applied this process in Luke 24:27. Take a moment to read Luke 24:13-32 in your Bible and observe the CONTEXT of this passage.

Where is Jesus walking?

_____

Who is He talking to?

_____

Then read verse 27:

*Beginning with Moses and all the Prophets, he **explained** to them what was said in all the Scriptures concerning himself.*

What verb is used to describe Jesus' process (see bold word)?

_____

How much of the Scriptures did Jesus include in His explanation?

_____

Your job is to interpret (or explain) what you understand God is saying in His Word—first for yourself and your own benefit, and then to benefit others.

No excuses. If you view the Bible as mostly impossible to understand, then you might think you have an excuse for giving up. Or you might wrongfully conclude that the Bible is a strange collection of stories and mysterious sayings that have no meaning.

But does this kind of thinking make sense? Why would God give you a book about Himself and how to live your life, yet make it hard for you to understand it? The answer is that He didn't! God meant for men and women of all ages, including a guy like you, to be able to understand the Bible. You don't have to wait until you are older. And you don't need to wait for an "expert" to help you.

No, God wants you to know His Word...*now*. God wants you to understand as much as you can. Then you can start making the right kinds of choices right away. The issue is not *can* you understand the Bible. The issue is do you *want* to understand the Bible? It's up to you. Your mission is to understand the meaning of what you read in your Bible.

What is your most common excuse for not reading your Bible more often, and what will you do about it?

_____

_____

_____

G row in your understanding. How does a person grow mentally? When you were younger, you began by reading simple books with simple words, such as "See Spot run." You learned to do simple math, such as "One plus one equals two." Growing in your understanding of your Bible takes the same basic efforts. In this book, you are learning the basic tools that will equip you to understand your Bible. And this is just the beginning. What does God command you to do for the rest of your life?

Grow in the grace and knowledge of our Lord and Savior Jesus Christ (2 Peter 3:18).

Grow in _____

Grow in _____

Who is to be the subject of your growth?

_____

THE BIBLE IS...
a Book You Can Understand

Great job—you have made it all the way through this chapter. Here's a high-five meant just for you! You have moved forward on the noble quest to understand your Bible better. In fact, it is the most important quest ever—one that not very many people take.

Why? Because most people aren't willing to pay the price that is required to unlock the epic mysteries of God. Some recognize that the challenges are great and choose not to start the journey. Others start out quickly, but then they become distracted or discouraged and lose sight of their goal. Those who don't make this effort don't realize that they are missing out on the joy and success that comes with understanding the Bible.

I hope you now realize the importance of understanding your Bible. My prayer is that you are already seeing spiritual growth take place in your life. But this growth is only the beginning. It's like the uppermost tip of an iceberg. There is so much more that you can and will learn in the future. You have a lifetime of discovery ahead of you.

You may have heard this saying: "Give a man a fish, and you feed him for a day. Teach him how to fish, and you feed him for a lifetime." That is what learning how to understand the Bible is all about—it's like learning how to catch fish. So hang in there. Commit yourself to finishing this book. There are a lot more fish to be caught!

★ Understanding Your Bible ★

In this chapter you looked at what is involved in understanding the M-E-A-N-I-N-G of what the authors of the Bible originally wrote. On this page, write out the point of each letter. (I'll get you started with "M.")

Meanings are always plain or obvious

E_____

A_____

N_____

I_____

N_____

G_____

Write out one thing you liked, learned, or want to do to better understand God's instructions to you in His Word, the Bible.

_____

_____

The Bible Is...
a Book That Will Change Your Life

7

Nobody likes change. Well, at least most of the time we don't. For example, you love your summer break, and hate having to change from sleeping in, playing with your friends, going swimming, and staying up late when summer break is over and it's back-to-school time. What a shock you receive on the first day of school! Everything changes. One day you're doing cool things with the neighbor kids, without a care in the world—and the next day, you are sitting in a classroom and having to do homework.

But change is a part of life. A lot of times change is hard, but it is usually for the better.

Now, are you ready for a good kind of change—that is, another step toward gaining a better understanding of your Bible? This step has to do with applying God's truths to your life. As the chapter title says, the Bible is a book that will change your life!

Here's how it works: After you have read a verse or passage in your Bible—after you have observed it, asked your questions, checked everything out, and grasped what it means—*then* you must ask and answer the question, "How can I put this information into action in my life?"

This is *application*—the final step in Bible study. It is at this point that you apply what you've learned and put it to work in your daily life.

Fun in God's Word!

Reading your Bible is not just about increasing your knowledge of God's Word, like knowing where to find the different books in the Bible. The ultimate goal of your Bible reading is all about bringing change to your life. The reason God gave you the Bible is to help you grow more and more like Jesus. So that should be the focus of your time in God's Word—letting it influence your thoughts, words, and actions.

Have your pen handy and, of course, your Bible, so you can write down the answers to the questions on the next few pages as we look in God's Word and spell out A-P-P-L-Y.

Applying starts with reading. I know I've already said this before, but it's true. You cannot apply God's Word in your life until you know what it says. This means you need to read carefully, using the step called OBSERVATION. Here's a quick review of this step: As you read a passage, you are to ask questions like...

Who are the people in the passage?

What are they doing?

Where is this story or verse taking place? In what location?

When is this taking place? Is it morning, evening, or...?

Then you move to the next step, which is INTERPRETATION. In this step you use the 3 "Cs" of CONTEXT, CULTURE, and CROSS-REFERENCES to learn more about what you are reading:

Context—This is determined by reading the verses or paragraphs immediately before and after the verse or paragraph you are studying. Looking at context will answer most of your questions about a passage of Scripture.

Culture—Just as you live in a modern-day culture with jet planes, fast cars, the Internet, TV, and video games, the people of the Bible lived in a culture of camels, donkeys, small fishing boats, and farming as a way of life. That is culture.

Cross-References—So that you can better understand a verse or passage, you want to read other verses or passages that are similar. Most Bibles have notes next to the words or phrases in your passage that refer you to other scriptures that help explain the passage you are studying. For instance, if you want to learn more about sheep or shepherds, you can read many different verses that will help answer your questions.

The next step is to APPLY what you have learned. Here are some questions you can ask to discover how a verse or passage could be applied in your life:

Question #1—Is there an example for me to follow?

Read Daniel 1:5 and 8 below which describes a decision Daniel had to make.

The king assigned them a daily amount of food and wine from the king's table. They were to be trained for three years, and after that they were to enter the king's service...But Daniel resolved not to defile himself with the royal food and wine, and he asked the chief official for permission not to defile himself this way.

Application: How can I follow Daniel's example and do what is right at school?

Write a brief application here:

_____

_____

_____

_____

Question #2—Is there a promise from God?

What is Jesus' promise in the verse that follows?

Surely I [Jesus] am with you always, to the very end of the age (Matthew 28:20).

Application: How can this promise help me when I feel unsure or like I'm all alone?

_____

_____

_____

Question #3—*Is there a warning for me to listen to?*

What is the warning in this verse?

Flee the evil desires of youth and pursue righteousness, faith, love and peace, along with those who call on the Lord out of a pure heart (2 Timothy 2:22).

_____

_____

Application: How can I apply this warning the next time my buddies want me to do something I know is wrong? Write a brief application here:

_____

_____

_____

Question #4—*Is there a command to obey?*

What is the double command that follows the warning in 2 Timothy 2:22 below?

Flee the evil desires of youth and

pursue righteousness, faith, love and peace,

along with those who call on the Lord out of a pure heart
(2 Timothy 2:22).

Command #1: What things am I to avoid?

_____

_____

Command #2: What things am I to pursue?

_____

_____

With what kinds of people?

_____

_____

Application: How can I apply these commands as I choose my friends?

_____

_____

Where would I most likely find kids "who call on the Lord out of a pure heart"?

_____

More application: God wants you to avoid making friends with kids who get into trouble and find friends who love Him. What attitude should you have, then, about attending youth activities at your church?

_____

_____

Proper understanding provides the right application—What happens when you misunderstand your schoolteacher's instructions before taking a test? Disaster, right? Well, the same can happen when you misunderstand the Bible. You cannot do what God wants you to do if you don't clearly understand what He's asking of you.

What is God's clear, hard-to-miss, double command in Ephesians 6:1-2?

1 *Children, obey your parents in the Lord, for this is right.*

2 *"Honor your father and mother"—which is the first commandment with a promise.*

Command #1:_____

_____

Command #2:_____

_____

Application: How should you apply these clear commands the next time your mom asks you to clean up your room or help your brother or sister?

_____

_____

Personalize your problems—God is a personal God. He cares about you, and therefore He has written the Bible with you in mind. He wants your personal obedience and loyalty. Many of His promises apply to you. Don't think that the Bible doesn't apply to you. When you read the Bible, think in terms of "I," "me," and "mine."

Look at Jesus' command below and write out how you can apply it by using the word "I" in your application.

Love the Lord your God with all your heart and with all your soul and with all your mind (Matthew 22:37).

Personal application: What can I do to show that I love God with all my heart and all my soul and all my mind? (One hint: Be more faithful to read His Word.) Jot down several other ways can you show God your love for Him.

_____

_____

_____

_____

Limit your application—Don't overwhelm yourself by trying to apply too many things from your Bible at one time. Instead, be selective. Select just one or two applications that you know God wants you to work on right now, today.

A good way to limit what you apply is to ask yourself, "What is my #1 problem?" You probably know the answer to this already! For instance,

Do you have a problem with obeying your parents?

Do you tell lies?

Do you get angry?

Whatever that #1 problem is, write it in this space.

_____

_____

This will help you focus on the most urgent need in your life right now. What does God say you should do about this problem? Circle the problems God mentions in the verse that follows:

Rid yourselves of all malice and all deceit, hypocrisy, envy, and slander of every kind (1 Peter 2:1).

Malice means desiring to inflict harm or suffering on another person.

Deceit means concealing or altering the truth.

Hypocrisy means being phony—pretending to be something you are not.

Envy means wanting what someone else has.

Slander means making up false or evil stories about another person.

Which one of these areas of sin do you think God wants you to work on right now?

_____

_____

As always, once you have identified a problem you need to work on, you must do something about it. What will you do to bring about change? And, what will you do today?

_____

_____

Your goal is change—Personal application of God's Word will help you reach your goal of spiritual growth and change. The questions below will help you to apply truths that bring about change. As you read or study your Bible, ask yourself: How does what I am reading relate to...

...my relationship with God?

...my relationships with family members?

...my relationships with others?

Then ask yourself: What changes do I need to make in my behavior so that these relationships can be more pleasing to God?

THE BIBLE IS...
a Book That Will Change Your Life

Application comes in all shapes and sizes. Sometimes your application will require you to do one specific thing, like returning a library book that's overdue. Or it could call for you to apologize to your sister for being mean to her, or to say, "Sorry, Mom," after you give her a hard time.

At other times your application will take time and effort, like breaking the habit of lying. Or it may require taking a series of steps, like making weekly payments out of your allowance to replace something you broke while goofing off or something you borrowed and lost.

Applications that deal with external actions (like lying, stealing, yelling) can be stopped at any time with a simple act of obedience. But heart attitudes and motives can be harder to fix because they require internal change—that is, change in your mind and heart. This kind of application goes deeper and calls for you to let God work in your heart so you will want to do what is right. Ask God for His help as you work on making change happen. He is always glad to help you!

★ Understanding Your Bible ★

In this chapter, we have looked at an important reason why you want to understand your Bible. You must first understand what God is asking you to do so you can obey and A-P-P-L-Y His commands in your life. On this page, write out the point of each letter below. (I'll get you started with "A.")

Application starts with reading

P_____

P_____

L_____

Y_____

Write out one thing you liked, learned, or want to do to better understand God's instructions to you in His Word, the Bible.

_____

_____

The Bible Is...
a Book Filled with Treasure

8

Part 1

What are some things you would do when you go to the ocean and play on the beach? You can plunge into the surf, run in the water along the shore, or fly a kite. You can also build sand castles. If you were to build a large sand castle, you would need a shovel to help scoop up all the sand needed for the structure.

Imagine that as you are digging, you uncover a buried treasure of some sort. At some time in the past, a person had lost jewelry or coins that had become covered by the waves and tide until they were buried in the sand. You end up being so excited about your discovery that you forget all about working on your sand castle.

Well, as a fellow Bible student, my prayer is that you would know the same kind of excitement as you discover more of the treasure to be found in God's Word. In fact, I hope you are so thrilled about taking time to understand your Bible that you will want to read it every day.

Having the Right Attitude

Are you ready to do something a little different in these next two chapters? Get your pen or pencil handy, and, of course, your Bible. Together we will look at eight steps that can lead you further along in the joy of discovery that comes from "digging up" the treasures in God's Word.

It's fairly easy to be committed to Bible study when someone is looking over your shoulder, or when you are doing your lessons along with a group of other guys in a Sunday school class. But the real test of your desire and commitment to know God will come when you are all by yourself. It's helpful when you are accountable to a leader or other friends. But what will happen when it is just you, your Bible, and God?

Right now I want to encourage you to develop an attitude that desires to continue reading God's Word. This attitude that will affect everything you do for the rest of your life—and it can start today! More specifically, I am talking about the attitude of *desire*.

A desire to know God. In this book, you have already learned what you must do to understand your Bible better. But none of this will happen unless you have a real desire or hunger for God that can only be satisfied by studying His Word.

Where does this desire come from? It must come from within you—from your heart. No parent, no Sunday school leader, and no pastor can give you this longing. If you have a thirst to know God and His truths, you will want to read and study the Bible over and over, day after day. You will feel a need to know and understand God and His message to you.

What illustration did the psalmist use in Psalm 42:1-2 to describe his feelings about knowing God?

> *As the deer pants for streams of water,*
> *so my soul pants for you, my God.*
> *My soul thirsts for God, for the living God.*

The deer: _____

_____

Your soul is to: _____

_____

_____

What words did the apostle Paul use to convey his passion for God?

I want to know Christ—yes, to know the power of his resurrection (Philippians 3:10).

_____

_____

To know God with such great desire and passion requires that you have a hunger to understand your Bible. Why the Bible? Because it is in the Bible that God reveals Himself to us. God also reveals Himself through His Son, Jesus Christ, whose life and ministry are described for us in the Bible.

Words like *desiring, hungering, thirsting,* and *craving* describe a heart attitude. And for you to develop this kind of attitude is a choice! Do you want to know Jesus? Choose to read about Him in your Bible. As Jerome, an early church father noted,

> Ignorance of the Bible means ignorance of Christ.

Eight Steps to Developing a Right Attitude for the Bible

Why is it that on some Saturday mornings, you are willing to get up early instead of sleeping in? Or why are there times when you are willing to spend extra hours perfecting a skill? The answer is found in one word: *desire*.

When you have a desire to do something well—whether it is being a fast swimmer, or getting the best score on a video game, or being able to pin down your older brother when you wrestle—you will do whatever is necessary to become good. You will set goals and work hard to reach them.

There are some time-tested steps you can take to reach the goal of knowing God better. As you read them, you'll notice some are familiar because we looked at them earlier. But that's okay because it's easy to forget what we learned, right?

As we begin, here's a brief prayer you may want to pray: "God, please burn these steps into my heart and mind so that they will become lifelong habits. Amen."

Step #1—*Hear the Bible taught*. Most kids sit in church or youth group or a Sunday school class and "hear" the Word of God preached and taught, but few of them really listen to what is being said. How can a person hear but not listen?

Jesus spoke a parable in Luke 8:4-15 about the Word of God—about the Bible. In the parable, Jesus compared those who heard and responded to the Word of God to those who didn't hear and therefore did not respond. Be sure you read the whole parable in your Bible later. But for now, take a look at verse 15 below. Describe the kind of heart that hears *and* responds.

> *The seed on good soil stands for those with a noble and good heart, who hear the word, retain it, and by persevering produce a crop.*

What kind of heart is described here?

_____

What actions indicate a person with this kind of heart?

— _____

— _____

— _____

What is the end product of such a person's efforts?

_____

Application: What should your prayer be each time you go to church?

_____

_____

According to the verse below, how does God help you when His Word is being taught?

Ears that hear and eyes that see—the LORD has made them both (Proverbs 20:12).

_____

_____

Translated into your everyday language, this means, "Pay attention and stay awake!"

A Tip for Hearing

To remember and use what you hear preached and taught, take notes. Ask your Dad or Mom for a cool notebook. Then take it with you to church, youth group, and Sunday school. And don't forget to take your pen as well so you can write down what is being taught.

A Boy's Guide to Discovering His Bible

Step #2—*Find a time and place to study God's Word.*
The world is noisy! As you are reading this book, you probably hear cars driving by, sirens wailing, the TV or some other electronic device blaring, and people talking. It's hard to pay attention when there are all kinds of background noises, isn't it?

That's why it's important for you to find a quiet place—a place where you can spend time alone with God. Maybe it's mission impossible for you to find such a place, but making an effort to do this will show you are serious about getting to know God better. Read the verse below and write *when* and *where* Abraham, a great man and the father of the Jewish nation, met with God.

> *Early...Abraham got up and returned to the place where he had stood before the LORD* (Genesis 19:27).

When? _____

Where? _____

When did King David, the greatest leader in the history of ancient Israel, meet with God, and what was his attitude? David wrote:

O God, You are my God;
Early will I seek You;
My soul thirsts for You;
My flesh longs for You
In a dry and thirsty land
Where there is no water (Psalm 63:1 NKJV).

When? _____

His desire? _____

_____

How about Jesus, God in human flesh? What seemed to be Jesus' practice in Mark 1:31?

Very early in the morning, while it was still dark, Jesus got up, left the house and went off to a solitary place, where he prayed.

When? _____

_____

Where? _____

_____

What did he do? _____

Should you get up early or not? I'm not saying you must get up early. And the Bible does not command you to do that either. However, it seems from these examples—and probably from your own experience—that if you don't get up even just a little early each day to spend time with God, you probably will not get around to it all day long. Again, your success in meeting with God goes right back to your desire. How much do you really want to get to know God? Again, it's your choice!

Step #3—*Take time to pray.* For a guy your age, praying to God might not be something you've had a lot of practice doing. Maybe you take turns praying around the kitchen table at home (when Mom and Dad ask you to), or say grace several times a week, or with your friends at church (when your teacher asks you to). But do you ever spend any time praying alone—just because *you* want to or need to?

This may be something new for you, or even a little scary. But prayer is simply talking to God. It's telling Him about your upcoming day, asking Him for His help on a test you will be taking or for dealing with a difficult kid at school. Prayer is also telling God you're sorry for lying to your mom or dad about finishing your homework last night just so you could play your new video game.

Like any good thing and worthy pursuit, prayer requires a decision and takes effort. If you're not praying—or not praying very much!—run through this checklist:

Check your desire. Here we go again—we are right back to attitude. More specifically, *your* attitude. Prayer will never become a wonderful habit if the one main ingredient—desire—is missing. You might already know what you should do—pray. And you might already know why you should pray—to talk to God. But if you don't desire to pray, it won't become real in your life.

What does Psalm 119:164 tell you about David's prayer life and his desire to pray?

Seven times a day I praise you for your righteous laws.

_____

Application: Maybe a first step for you into starting to pray would be to set a goal to praise God seven times a day. Just take a moment to say, "God, thank You for _____."

Check your understanding of sin. Prayer and Bible study are spiritual exercises. They require a heart that is clean. This is another reason why you should pray. You keep your heart clean by confessing your sins to God through prayer. Sin is anything that does not please God. What does this verse say happens when you do not confess your sin? Or put another way, why is confessing sin so important?

If I had cherished sin in my heart, the Lord would not have listened (Psalm 66:18).

_____

_____

Check your relationship with God. Is there some bad behavior that is creating a barrier between you and God? Have you been mean to someone? Did you lie to your parents? Did you cheat at school? Whatever you have done that you know was wrong, bow your head and your heart, and admit it to God. Ask Him to forgive you and help you stop it. Don't let sin put a wall between you and your relationship with God.

The apostle Paul said you are to get rid of wrong habits. What bad habit is mentioned in Ephesians 4:29?

Do not let any unwholesome talk come out of your mouths, but only what is helpful for building others up according to their needs, that it may benefit those who listen.

_____

_____

What are you to do instead?

_____

_____

To wrap up Step #3—take time to pray, and always remember: Something is better than nothing. Start with a few minutes when you get up each morning. Think and pray through your day. Are you facing a test? Pray for wisdom for the test. How about your after-school athletic activity? Pray for godly conduct at the sporting event, especially if you lose! And you should always pray to have a good attitude toward your parents.

We will continue on with the remaining steps in the next chapter. See you there!

THE BIBLE IS...
a Book Filled with Treasure

Think again about going to the beach. What was the reason you found the buried treasure? It was because you started digging in the sand, right? Without digging, you would not have found the treasure. There would have been no exciting discovery. That's the way it is with discovering the truths in God's Word. You will never experience the joy of discovery until you start digging into your Bible for answers:

—answers about God

—answers about your salvation

—answers about your attitude

—answers about your conduct

The answer to every question you will ever have can be found in your Bible. Shouldn't this motivate you to desire to understand your Bible?

★ Understanding Your Bible ★

In this chapter you looked at three steps you can take to know more about God. These steps may be new to you. Or maybe you have been a little slow to apply them. Review them now by writing out the three steps presented in this chapter:

Step #1—

Step #2—

Step #3—

Write out one thing you liked, learned, or want to do to better understand God's instructions to you in His Word, the Bible.

_____

_____

_____

_____

The Bible Is...
a Book Filled with Treasure

Part 2

9

Are you are a big fan of comic books? They have have been extremely popular for many years. But that might be changing with all of the comic book superhero characters moving into cartoons created for TV or video. Believe it or not, in the past kids your age saved money from their allowances so they could go to the store and buy the latest edition of their favorite comic book hero. As a result, today there are a lot of used as well as new comic books floating around. I recently read about an old comic book that was found hidden in the wall of a house that was being torn down. Because it was so rare and in great condition, the comic book was sold for a *very* large amount of money!

It's hard to believe that a comic book could have such enormous value. It shows us the extraordinary value the world puts on meaningless fantasy. I say that because comic book superheroes aren't even real people. And the stories are made up—they don't really happen.

But the Bible, by contrast, is worth infinitely more—and

it is filled with centuries of stories of superheroes who really lived. Your Bible is not full of fantasy. It is full of heroes just as exciting as any comic book character and loaded with truths that really can change you and help you do well in life. It shows you how you—yes *you!*—can be a superhero.

How Much Do You Value Your Bible?

If your pen and Bible are handy, get ready to continue looking at the eight steps we began in the previous chapter—eight steps that can help you increase the joy that comes from getting into God's Word.

In the last chapter we imagined finding hidden treasure buried in the sand on the beach. Do you realize that Jesus spoke about discovering hidden treasure, about finding something of great value? The Bible tells us He actually spoke a parable about finding treasure.

Hopefully you remember what you learned about parables in an earlier chapter. Parables are stories that illustrate important information Jesus wanted people to understand. Jesus used familiar objects or events to illustrate His points. In many of the parables, Jesus used the word "like" to describe what He was talking about. Let's look at two of Jesus' parables.

Parable #1: In the verse below, circle the word "like" and underline the words "the kingdom of heaven."

> *The kingdom of heaven is like treasure hidden in a field. When a man found it, he hid it again, and then in his joy went and sold all he had and bought that field* (Matthew 13:44).

What did Jesus say the kingdom of heaven is like?

_____

What does Jesus say the man in this story did when he found a treasure as special as the kingdom of heaven?

_____

_____

What emotion did this man experience when he discovered this treasure of the kingdom of heaven?

_____

Parable #2: In the verses below, circle the word "like" and underline the words "the kingdom of heaven."

Again, the kingdom of heaven is like a merchant looking for fine pearls. When he found one of great value, he went away and sold everything he had and bought it (Matthew 13:45-46).

What did Jesus say the kingdom of heaven is like?

_____

_____

What does Jesus say the man in this story did when he found a treasure as special as the kingdom of heaven?

_____

_____

In both parables, Jesus is saying that knowing and wanting to be near God—in "the kingdom of heaven"—is the most important thing anyone could want. It is a place of priceless value. A person should be willing to do whatever it takes and give up everything he possesses to make sure he can be close to God.

Here's a thought: These two parables talk about something of great value. Nothing is more valuable than having a book like the Bible that tells you how to live as God's child here on earth and with God later in heaven.

Eight Steps to Developing a Right Attitude for the Bible

Are you beginning to grasp the importance of your Bible? You cannot see God physically, but when you read His Word, you gain knowledge and understanding about how to know Him personally through His Son, Jesus Christ.

If you see the Bible as a key way to get close to God, then you will make a habit of following the eight steps in the last chapter and this one. First, here are the three steps we looked at in the previous chapter:

Step #1—Hear the Bible taught.

Step #2—Choose a time and place to study God's Word.

Step #3—Take time to pray.

Now we're ready to look at the next five steps:

Step #4—*Read the Bible.* Reading your Bible is more important than just listening to the Bible being taught. When you hear a Bible story, you remember some of the story. But no matter how hard you try to listen, you will still miss and forget a lot. But when you *read* that same story on your own, you are more likely to remember it.

Earlier, in chapter 4, we discussed *how* you are to read your Bible. Now let's see *why*—why should you read your Bible? Deuteronomy 17:19-20 lists four life-changing effects that would occur in the life of any king of Israel who read God's word. In the verses below, circle the word "that" each time it occurs. Then underline what follows to discover the benefits of reading God's Word.

> *It [God's Word] shall be with him, and he [the king] shall read it all the days of his life,*
>
> *that he may learn to fear the LORD his God and be careful to observe all the words of this law and these statutes,*
>
> *that his heart may not be lifted [in pride] above his brethren,*
>
> *that he may not turn aside from the commandment to the right hand or to the left, and*
>
> *that he may prolong his days in his kingdom, he and his children in the midst of Israel* (NKJV).

God knew that when a new king (usually a young man a little older than you) read and copied the Bible, it would have a profound effect on him. Every one of these benefits is a reason why you too should want to read your Bible. Which one is your favorite or the one you need or want most?

_____

_____

_____

Which Bible Translation Should You Read?

The Bible was originally written mostly in two languages, Hebrew and Greek. So the Bible you are using today was translated from those languages. Because God has preserved His Word through time with the help of careful scribes and translators, you can be sure your Bible is completely accurate and trustworthy.

The answer to the question, "Which Bible version should you read?" really comes down to which version is easiest for you to read and understand. Ask your parents to help you find the version that is clearest for you and will make you want to read and study God's Word.

And remember: It's never too early or too late to start reading the Bible. Dr. Harry Ironside, respected pastor and Bible student, when he was 14 years old, was concerned over not having read through the Bible as many times as he was years old. By the time he was 21 he had caught up. Later in life he was far ahead.

Here's a practical first step: If you are finding it hard to follow what is happening in the Old Testament, why not start with five minutes a day reading from the life of Jesus in Mark or Luke in the New Testament? The life of Jesus is a good place to begin—and you'll never be the same once you start following His example for how to live.

Step #5—*Study it.* The book of Proverbs speaks often about finding wisdom. For you to gain the wisdom of God doesn't just happen. You have to make an effort and search for it, dig it out, and understand it.

What four activities are involved in gaining wisdom, according to Proverbs 2:3-4?

3 [If you] call out for insight

and cry aloud for understanding,

4 and if you look for it as for silver

and search for it as for hidden treasure...

1.＿＿＿＿＿＿＿＿＿＿＿＿＿＿＿＿＿＿＿＿＿＿＿＿

2.＿＿＿＿＿＿＿＿＿＿＿＿＿＿＿＿＿＿＿＿＿＿＿＿

3.＿＿＿＿＿＿＿＿＿＿＿＿＿＿＿＿＿＿＿＿＿＿＿＿

4.＿＿＿＿＿＿＿＿＿＿＿＿＿＿＿＿＿＿＿＿＿＿＿＿

What are the two results you can gain from efforts?

5...then you will understand the fear of the LORD
and find the knowledge of God.

You will _____

_____

and_____

_____

What is the source of all of this information and these blessings?

6 The LORD gives wisdom,
from his mouth come knowledge and understanding.

_____

_____

According to the verse below, what term is used to describe a student of the Bible "who correctly handles the word of truth"?

Do your best to present yourself to God as one approved, a workman who does not need to be ashamed and who correctly handles the word of truth (2 Timothy 2:15).

He is called a _____ _____ _____ _____

_____ _____ _____ _____ .

Using a Study Bible

There are special study Bibles available to you that have lots of notes and helpful resources in them. You will grow in your understanding of God's Word when you use a study Bible. Ask your parents, pastor, or youth leader for their recommendations about which study Bible might be best for you. Or, you could ask your parents to take you to your local Christian bookstore so you can see the different study Bibles for yourself and ask the store clerk about them. You could also look on the Internet at the different options.

Step #6—*Memorize it.* If you are like most kids, you have no problem at all memorizing information you are interested in. For example, you can probably name every player on your favorite sports team. And if you are into action figures, you can probably name all your favorites and what they can do. Well, that's how easy and natural it can be to memorize God's Word. When something is important to you, you will make an effort to remember it.

According to Psalm 119:11, what does a young man do to defend himself against sin?

I have hidden your word in my heart that I might not sin against you.

_____

_____

Why Memorize God's Word?

There are some who say that after 24 hours, you may accurately remember up to:

5 percent of what you hear

15 percent of what you read

35 percent of what you study

100 percent of what you memorize

Step #7—*Think about it.* There is a kind of thinking that is called "meditation." This means taking time repeatedly during the day to remember the things you have read in God's Word and how they apply to your life. Would you like to be smarter than your teachers? Yes? Then read the verse below. What is God's promise if you take some time during each day to think or meditate on the Word of God?

I have more insight than all my teachers,

for I meditate [think] on your statutes [the Bible] (Psalm 119:97).

_____

_____

Step #8—*Live it.* The Bible is not a textbook to be read, studied, and then forgotten. God did not give you His Word just to inform you, but for you to respond to it. God gave you His instructions and commands so you would live by them. God wants you to be transformed—changed from the inside out—by what you read and study in the Bible.

The whole reason for this book about understanding your Bible is to give you tools that will help you understand God's instructions. Then you can correctly respond to His will for your life. What are the two options you face in your life, according to Romans 12:2?

Do not conform to the pattern of this world,
but be transformed by the renewing of your mind.

Option #1 _____

_____

Option #2 _____

_____

This verse (Romans 12:2) continues on. If you choose Option #2, what happens? Or, what is the result?

Then you will be able to test and approve what God's will is—
his good, pleasing and perfect will.

_____

_____

Please don't choose Option #1. It leads down the terrible road of rebellion and sin. Instead, choose Option #2. This choice will transform or change you as the Holy Spirit changes your thinking. When you think constantly about what is written in the Bible, you will desire more and more to live your life in a way that pleases God.

THE BIBLE IS...
a Book Filled with Treasure

Do you ever become uneasy when you don't know what's expected of you? For example, you would become nervous if you walked into class and your teacher handed you a test to take—without giving you any instructions. You need to know what is expected of you so you can do well on the test.

And whether you will admit it or not, you feel more comfortable when your parents clearly communicate their rules to you. You might not always want to obey their rules, but it is definitely helpful to know what is expected of you and your behavior.

That should give you some idea of the wonderful treasure you have in your Bible. In the Bible, God not only gives you instructions—He also gives you the answers for "taking the test of life." Can you believe it? God has given you *everything* you need for a godly life (2 Peter 1:3).

Choose to pick up your Bible, read through it, mine its treasures, and most importantly, live it. As a result, God will bless you. Your parents will be happy and proud of you. And you will be growing into a godly and wise and successful man.

★ Understanding Your Bible ★

We have finished looking at some time-tested steps you can take to get to know God better. And the more you turn these steps into habits, the more you will grow spiritually.

To review the steps again, write them out in the order you covered them in this chapter:

Step #4—

Step #5—

Step #6—

Step #7—

Step #8—

Write out one thing you liked, learned, or want to do to better understand God's instructions to you in His Word, the Bible.

_____

_____

_____

The Bible Is...
a Book with One Central Theme

10

Can you believe it? You are at the end—or at least the final chapter—of this book and your journey into understanding your Bible. If we were face-to-face, believe me, I'd be giving you a pat on the back and an enthusiastic high-five. You and I would be planning a celebration, maybe a trip for pizza or ice cream—or both!

By now you have picked up on why you should study your Bible. It is not just an old book from the past. As you've personally looked into it and made many life-changing applications, it has become so much more than white pages and black ink with a whole lot of words.

No, the Bible takes great care to let you know over and over again that it is the Word of God. It claims to be authored by God Himself. And it contains a message of utmost importance—a message that offers life not just for the present, but for all eternity. This makes the Bible special and one-of-a-kind, something definitely worth your time, attention, and study. As you understand God's message, you come to know

God Himself. And the more you read His message, the more you get to know what He desires to do for you.

Fun in God's Word!

And what is God's message? The whole Bible is built around the fascinating story of Jesus Christ and His promise of eternal life for those who accept Him as Savior and Lord. The main reason for finding out what the Bible says is to understand, know, believe in, and wholeheartedly follow Jesus. So let's look at Jesus. As always, you will need to have a pen handy, and of course your Bible, so you can write down some answers as we look in the Bible and spell out J-E-S-U-S.

Jesus is prophesied in the Old Testament. The type of Bible literature known as *prophecy* deals with future events. The books of Isaiah through Malachi in the Old Testament are largely about prophecy. When it comes to the prophecies of Jesus the Messiah, most of these books predicted and described Jesus' birth, life, and even His death. The Old Testament set the stage with its predictions for the first coming of Jesus.

Isaiah was one of the greatest Old Testament prophets. Seven hundred years before the birth of Jesus, Isaiah gave an amazing prophecy. Underline each descriptive name given of this child who was to come:

To us a child is born, to us a son is given, and the government will be on his shoulders. And he will be called Wonderful

Counselor, Mighty God, Everlasting Father, Prince of Peace (Isaiah 9:6).

The prophet Micah proclaimed the following incredible facts 700 years before Jesus' birth. Where did Micah predict Jesus would be born?

Bethlehem Ephrathah, though you are small among the clans of Judah, out of you will come for me one who will be ruler over Israel, whose origins are from of old, from ancient times (Micah 5:2).

_____

What does the New Testament say happened in a little town called Bethlehem?

Joseph also went up from the town of Nazareth in Galilee to Judea, to Bethlehem the town of David, because he belonged to the house and line of David. He went there to register with Mary, who was pledged to be married to him and was expecting a child. While they were there, the time came for the baby to be born (Luke 2:4-6)

_____

_____

Personal application: Do you have trust issues when it comes to believing what the Bible says? Think about your level of trust in God. How do these two fulfilled prophecies strengthen your trust in the Word of God?

_____

_____

_____

Entered the world for a reason. Why did Jesus come into this world? In chapter 1 of this book we looked at the story of Eve in Genesis 3. I'm sure you remember what happened to her. She disobeyed God's one and only rule and ate the forbidden fruit in the garden of Eden. That act of disobedience brought sin into the perfect world God created.

How are we to view sin? The world tells us sin is no big deal—it's nothing you need to worry about. You may have heard people say, "Hey, if it feels good, it must be okay."

But sin is extremely serious! In the Bible, sin is defined as anything that goes against God's holy standards in thought, word, or deed. And because God is holy, He must judge sin, just as God judged Adam and Eve's sin.

As you can see, anyone who sins has a very big problem with God. And just in case you think you are perfect, check out what the Bible says. How many people meet God's standard of perfection, according to this verse?

There is no one who does good, not even one (Romans 3:12).

_____

That brings us to the answer of the most important question of all: Why did Jesus come into the world? What answers does the Bible give?

God so loved the world that he gave his one and only Son, that whoever believes in him shall not perish but have eternal life (John 3:16).

_____

_____

The Son of Man [Jesus] came to seek and to save the lost (Luke 19:10).

_____

_____

Christ Jesus came into the world to save sinners (1 Timothy 1:15).

_____

Personal application: Only Jesus has ever been perfect. The rest of us cannot say that about ourselves, can we? Think back over this past week. How did you do sin-wise? I'm guessing you can think of several or even many times you failed and sinned. List just one thing that you know displeased God.

_____

_____

Even if you were to commit only one sin in your entire life, you would be a sinner. Every person has sinned, and that is the reason God sent His Son, Jesus Christ, to earth. Sin separates us from God, and through Jesus, we can come back to God again.

Sacrificed Himself for sinners. God is Spirit and cannot die. Christ, being God, took on a body of flesh and blood to make it possible for Him to die and pay the price for your sins. According to the verses that follow, what did Jesus' sacrificial death accomplish?

I have come that they may have life, and have it to the full (John 10:10).

— _____

— _____

Christ also suffered once for sins, the righteous for the unrighteous, to bring you to God (1 Peter 3:18).

_____

_____

Jesus' personal sacrifice demands a personal response. In the scriptures below, what should be your response toward Jesus?

To all who did receive him, to those who believed in his name, he gave the right to become children of God (John 1:12).

My response:_____

_____

Result:_____

_____

God presented Christ as a sacrifice of atonement [for sin]...to be received by faith (Romans 3:25).

My response:_____

_____

What are some results of deciding to receive Christ as Savior? Look to the **bold words** for your answers.

*God, who is rich in mercy, **made us alive with Christ** even when we were dead in transgressions* (Ephesians 2:4-5).

_____

_____

*Since we have been justified through faith, **we have peace with God** through our Lord Jesus Christ* (Romans 5:1).

_____

_____

Personal application: My friend, have you personally received Christ as your Savior and received His payment for your sin? If you have, pause and remember the significance of that life-changing decision. Then thank God with all your heart for making this possible for you.

If you have not received Christ as your Savior and received His payment for your sin, or you are not totally sure, take a moment now to pray. Tell God you want to know the truth, and you want to respond to what you have been studying—you want to receive Jesus as Savior and Lord.

If you are still not sure what to do, reach out and ask questions of those who can give you answers—a parent, a youth worker, a pastor. Or call out to Jesus as one man did in Mark 9:24 when he cried, *"Help me overcome my unbelief!"*

Ultimately, Jesus is coming again! The Bible is absolutely 100 percent reliable. God's prophets said Jesus, the Messiah, would come—and He did. But God isn't finished. There is more to come. The world is becoming more dark and desperate, but there is coming a day when Jesus will return and make things right. Bible scholars call this the study of last things, or as your pastor might call it, *eschatology*.

The night before Jesus was crucified, He announced what He would do when He returned to heaven. What was it?

My Father's house has many rooms; if that were not so, would I have told you that I am going there to prepare a place for you? (John 14:2).

_____

_____

What is Jesus going to do for all His followers when He comes back?

If I go and prepare a place for you, I will come back and take you to be with me that you also may be where I am (John 14:3).

_____

_____

Yes, it's true—Jesus said He was coming again! After Jesus rose from the dead and returned to heaven, two angels gave a promise about the future. What was their promise?

"Men of Galilee," they [the two angels] said, "why do you stand here looking into the sky? This same Jesus, who has been taken from you into heaven, will come back..." (Acts 1:11).

_____

_____

Personal application: The Bible is accurate in every single one of its predictions about Jesus' birth and Jesus' life. Therefore, you can trust that the Bible is just as accurate about Jesus' future return. With the promise that Jesus could return today, tomorrow, or later, the apostle Peter says in 2 Peter 3:11, *"You ought to live holy and godly lives."*

Personal application: What is one thing you could do tomorrow that would show your family and classmates that you are trying to live as Jesus wants you to?

_____

_____

_____

Showing Christlike behavior. One way to live a holy and godly life is to grow more like Jesus—to follow His example in as many ways as possible. Where will you find out how Jesus lived so you can live like Him? By reading about Jesus in your Bible and studying His life. Then, as you copy Jesus and pattern your life after His, you will be changed.

Here are three qualities to get you started in following His example:

Be a servant—Jesus left heaven and came to earth to die for your sins. What does Matthew 20:28 say was the purpose of Jesus' life?

The Son of Man did not come to be served, but to serve.

_____

Personal application: What is one thing can you do today or tomorrow to be a servant at home and at school?

_____

_____

Be a guy who prays—Look up these verses in your Bible. What was Jesus doing in each verse before He made important decisions, and what was the decision He had to make?

Luke 6:12-13—_____

_____

_____

Matthew 26:39-46—_____

_____

_____

Personal application: Prayer is simply talking to God. Even in a split second you can ask, in your mind, "Jesus, what is the right thing to do?" At every minute and in every situation, talking things over with Jesus helps. Trust Him—He wants to hear from you. As you think about the rest of your week, decide on a good time for spending some time talking to Jesus. Pick a time and write it here:

_____

Be good—Being good doesn't just happen. It doesn't come naturally. In fact, the opposite is what comes naturally! So you must make an effort to always do the right thing, like obeying your parents and telling the truth. What three steps does the following verse give for making the right choices and being good?

Flee the evil desires of youth and pursue righteousness, faith, love and peace, along with those who call on the Lord out of a pure heart (2 Timothy 2:22).

Run away from _____

Pursue _____

Associate with _____

THE BIBLE IS...
a Book with One Central Theme

The Bible is a life-changing book. And the primary purpose of Bible study is for you to understand what God wants you to do with your life. The ultimate goal of Bible study is not to merely circle or underline words, or fill in blanks, or make sure you know what happened before or after a particular verse.

No, the ultimate goal of Bible study is to have the Bible do something to *you*! That is why I wanted you to end your study looking at Jesus' life, drawing closer to Jesus, and worshiping Jesus. He—Jesus Christ—is the one theme of the Bible. The whole purpose of learning how to study the Bible is so all believers—including you—will imitate Jesus and follow His example.

I'm praying you will grasp how very special Jesus is as your Lord and Savior, and that you will see Him as the perfect model for how to live your life. The more you make the Bible a part of your life, the more you will want to live like Jesus.

★ Understanding Your Bible ★

In this concluding chapter we looked at the Person whom all the Bible is about—Jesus Christ. To help you remember the points from this chapter, write out the point of each letter. (I'll get you started with "J.")

Jesus is prophesied in the Old Testament

E_____

S_____

U_____

S_____

Write out one thing you liked, learned, or want to do to better understand God's instructions to you in His Word, the Bible.

_____

_____

Notes

1. Roy B. Zuck, *The Speaker's Quote Book*, citing J. Wilbur Chapman (Grand Rapids, MI: Kregel, 1997), p. 39

2. *God's Words for Life for Teens* (NIV) (Grand Rapids, MI: Inspirio, the Gift Group of Zondervan, 2000), p. 29.

Also by Jim George

A Boy After God's Own Heart

You've got a lot going on—school, activities, friends, and life at home. And you're taking on new challenges and opportunities which bring up important questions: How do you handle peer pressure and choose the right kind of friends? What if you're having a hard time doing your homework or getting along with your brothers and sisters? And what should you do when you mess up—especially with your parents or God?

The Bible has the answers to these questions and more. With God's help, you can...

- learn how to make good decisions and great friends
- see the benefits of homework and even chor
- get along better with your parents and other family members
- discover more about the Bible so you can grow closer to God

This book will take you on the most amazing journey you can experience—becoming a boy after God's own heart.

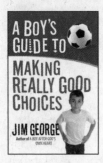

A Boy's Guide to Making Really Good Choices

Did you know that exercising your ability to make good choices is the biggest step you can take toward growing up? That's important because you make lots of decisions every day—

- What should I say...or not say?
- How should I spend my time right now?
- When will I do my schoolwork? My chores?
- Who should I choose as my friends?
- What should I wear...watch...read?

When you make good decisions, you'll do better with God, your parents, your friends, school, and everything else.

So start learning how to make the best kinds of choices... today!